LEVEL 2

Ruth

retold by
CAROL CHRISTIAN

© Copyright text Carol Christian 1996
© Copyright illustrations Macmillan Education Ltd 1996

All rights reserved. No reproduction, copy or transmission of
this publication may be made without written permission.

No paragraph of this publication may be reproduced, copied or
transmitted save with written permission or in accordance with
the provisions of the Copyright, Designs and Patents Act 1988,
or under the terms of any licence permitting limited copying issued
by the Copyright Licensing Agency, 90 Tottenham Court Road,
London W1P 9HE.

Any person who does any unauthorised act in relation to this
publication may be liable to criminal prosecution and civil
claims for damages.

First published 1996 by
MACMILLAN EDUCATION LTD
London and Basingstoke
*Associated companies and representatives in Accra, Banjul,
Cairo, Dar es Salaam, Delhi, Freetown, Gaborone, Harare,
Hong Kong, Johannesburg, Kampala, Lagos, Lahore, Lusaka,
Mexico City, Nairobi, São Paulo, Tokyo*

ISBN 0–333–63938–3

10 9 8 7 6 5 4 3 2
05 04 03 02 01 00 99 98 97 96

Printed in Hong Kong

A catalogue record for this book is available from the
British Library.

Illustrations by Ursula Sieger

Naomi and her husband Elimelech

Long, long ago a man called Elimelech lived with his wife Naomi and their two sons, Mahlon and Chilion, in Bethlehem, in the land of Judah.

He and his wife were part of a large family and had lots of relatives and friends in the town. Elimelech owned a piece of land on which he grew the food for his family.

But a time came when, for many seasons, there was no rain in Judah and the crops dried up in the fields. Many people were hungry. Naomi couldn't give her sons enough food to make them strong and healthy. Even the boys' names, Mahlon and Chilion, meant 'ill' and 'unhealthy'.

The family decides to leave Bethlehem

Elimelech and Naomi decided to leave their home in Bethlehem and go to the other side of the River Jordan, to find food for their family.

Travellers from the east told them, 'The land of Moab is richer and greener than the land of Judah. No one there is hungry. You'll be able to feed your children if you go there.'

Moab was only about sixty kilometres away, but people didn't travel much in those days. To Naomi and Elimelech, Moab was a foreign country, where people wore strange clothes and worshipped strange gods. They had never heard anything good about the people of Moab. However, they still decided to go.

'The women of Moab are beautiful,' people warned Naomi. 'They'll steal your husband, if they can.'

'Remember your God, the God of Israel,' people reminded Elimelech. 'Don't bow down to Baal and other idols, as the Moabites do.'

'You're very brave to go so far from home,' their friends and relatives said. 'Even if you get there safely, we shall never see you again. Are you sure you want to go and live among strangers?'

'Yes, we're sure,' said Elimelech. 'We must go, if we want to make a better life for our children.'

Elimelech and Naomi left Bethlehem with fear in their hearts. They said goodbye to everyone they had ever known. There were tears in their eyes as they set off with their sons for the land of Moab.

The years in Moab

For some years they did well in their new home. They had enough to eat. And the people of Moab were not as bad as they expected. They were no worse, and no better, than the people of Judah.

Then Elimelech died, leaving Naomi alone with their two sons. God had not given her any more sons or daughters.

Mahlon and Chilion grew up and married Moabite girls. Mahlon married Ruth and Orpah became Chilion's wife. Orpah and Ruth hoped to bear children, and Naomi hoped for grandchildren.

However, Mahlon and Chilion had never been strong. Before long, they, too, died. Naomi was now living in a foreign country, with no husband and no sons to support her.

The three widows tried to comfort one another. But, as a foreigner, Naomi had no rights in the land of Moab.

She said to her daughters-in-law, 'What shall I do now? I don't own any property. I have no relatives in Moab to help me. If I don't do something, we shall all starve to death.'

The girls hung their heads. It was true. There was little hope for three women who had neither husbands nor children.

Then a neighbour said,'Why don't you return to Bethlehem? Life is better there now. The Lord has provided food for his people at last. They have plenty of wheat and barley in their store houses. Even the name Bethlehem means "house of bread".

'Is that true?' asked Naomi. 'I didn't know that. I haven't seen my home in Judah for ten years. But what will happen to Orpah and Ruth?'

'Your daughters-in-law will be all right,' said the neighbour. 'They have families here in Moab who will take care of them. They'll find new husbands. They are beautiful young women.'

Naomi sets off for Judah

When Naomi decided to go home, Orpah and Ruth said at once, 'You can't travel all the way to Bethlehem by yourself. We'll come with you.'

The three women gathered their few possessions together and set off on the road to the land of Judah.

After a while, Naomi turned to Orpah and Ruth and said, 'You've come far enough, my daughters. Go back to your own mothers and your own homes. Perhaps the Lord will be as kind to you as you have been to me and my sons.'

She kissed them both goodbye, but they burst into tears and said, 'Please don't send us away. We are your family now.'

But Naomi said, 'Dry your tears, my dear daughters. Mahlon and Chilion are dead, but you're alive, and you're still young. You must try to find happiness, each of you, with a new husband.'

'No, no,' they said. 'We'll go back with you to your people.'

Naomi shook her head. 'Go home, my daughters. Your lives are not over yet. You'll marry and have children. I have no more sons for you to marry, and I'm too old to marry again. Even if I married and had sons, you couldn't wait for them to grow up. It isn't your fault that the Lord has turned against me.'

At these words her daughters-in-law began to weep again. Then Orpah said, 'Dear Naomi, what you say is true. We belong here with our own people.'

Ruth refuses to leave Naomi

Orpah kissed Naomi goodbye and turned back towards her home. Ruth, however, hugged Naomi tightly in her arms and refused to let her go.

Naomi said to her, 'Look at your sister-in-law, Orpah. She's returning to her people and her gods. Go back with her, Ruth. Your life is here in Moab.'

    But Ruth said to Naomi, 'Don't ask me to leave you or abandon you. Where you go, I will go, and where you stay, I will stay. Your people will be my people and your God will be my God. Where you die, I will die, and I'll be buried where you are buried. Nothing, not even death, can part me from you.'

    When Naomi saw that Ruth was determined to go with her, she said, 'My daughter, I won't say anything more.'

Naomi and Ruth arrive in Bethlehem

Naomi and Ruth travelled on together until they reached Bethlehem. The people of the town were astonished to see them. They welcomed Naomi with open arms.

'Is it really Naomi?' they cried.

'Don't call me Naomi,' she said sadly. 'Naomi means "pleasant". Call me Mara, which means "bitter". The Lord has made my life bitter. He has turned against me. I went away full, with a husband and two sons, but the Lord has taken them. He has brought me back empty.'

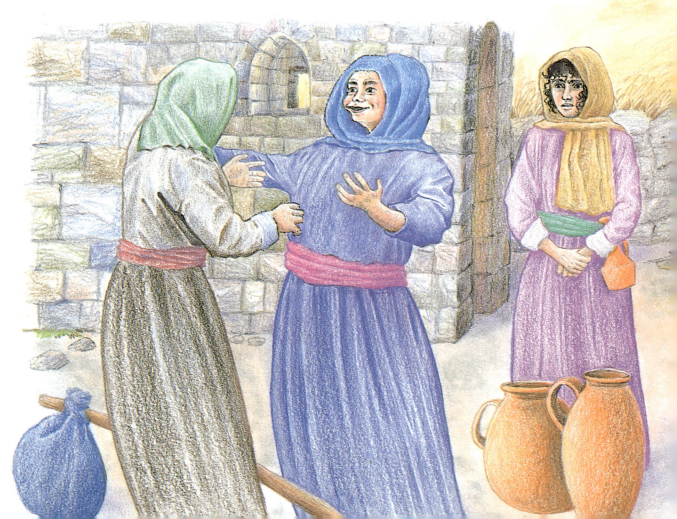

The people looked at Ruth but did not speak to her. They had never heard anything good about Moabite women.

Naomi returned home from Moab with Ruth, her Moabite daughter-in-law, just as the harvest began. Everyone was working in the fields to bring in the ripe barley.

Ruth goes to work in the fields

Ruth said to Naomi, 'Shall I go out into the fields and collect the grains of barley which the harvesters leave behind? Perhaps someone will be kind and allow me to gather any stalks that remain.'

It was the custom in those days to allow poor people to pick up the grains of barley left by the harvesters, before the birds ate them.

'Go and do that, my daughter,' said Naomi.

So Ruth went to a field and spoke to the overseer. 'Please, may I collect the grains that fall from the stalks of barley, as the harvesters gather them? And may I gather any stalks that remain?'

Boaz offers Ruth his protection

Now it happened that the field where Ruth was working belonged to a member of Elimelech's family, a rich man named Boaz. When he came to watch the harvesters at work, he saw the stranger in his field.
　'Who's that?' he asked his overseer.

'That's the Moabite girl who married Elimelech's son, Mahlon. She came back from Moab with Naomi,' the overseer replied. 'She asked for permission to collect the barley and has been working hard since early morning.'

Boaz went to speak to Ruth. 'My daughter,' he said, 'listen to me. Don't go into anyone else's fields to collect barley. It will be safer for you if you stay with my servant girls. Follow them into the fields where they are working. I've told my young men about you. No one will harm you. If you get thirsty, go and drink from the water jars my men have filled.'

Ruth bowed low, and touched her face to the ground. 'How have I earned such favours?' she asked. 'I am a foreigner in Bethlehem.'

Boaz answered, 'I know about your kindness to your mother-in-law, Naomi. Although your husband is dead, you left your mother and father and country and came to live among strangers. The Lord God of Israel is your God now. He'll take care of you.'

When the harvesters sat down to rest and eat their meal, Boaz called to her, 'Come and sit over here, near me. Take some bread and dip it in the wine.'

He offered her a handful of roasted barley. Ruth ate as much of it as she wanted and saved some to take home for Naomi.

When the workers returned to the fields, Boaz said to his men. 'The Moabite girl looks tired. Drop some full stalks of barley here and there, where she can pick them up, and don't scold her for taking them.'

Ruth worked until evening. When she removed the stalks, she had a huge bag full of barley.

Naomi is pleased to see the barley

Naomi was astonished when she saw the bag of barley. Then Ruth gave her the roasted barley she had saved from her meal.

'Where did you find all this?' Naomi asked. 'Someone has been very generous to you.'

'I worked in the field of a man called Boaz,' Ruth answered. 'He was very kind. He told me to stay with his servants and to work in his fields until the harvest is over.'

'The Lord is with him!' exclaimed Naomi. 'He has not forgotten his dead relative, Elimelech. He wants to help those who are still alive. Do as he told you, my daughter, and you will be safe from harm.'

Ruth continued to work with Boaz's servants until the barley and wheat harvests came to an end. Each night she went home to Naomi's house.

Naomi makes plans for Ruth

Naomi was making plans for Ruth. She saw that Boaz, who was a good man, admired her daughter-in-law. He was also a relative, a member of Elimelech's family, though he was not their closest relative.

Naomi and Ruth were living on Elimelech's piece of land. Naomi wanted to sell the land and give her daughter-in-law to the buyer in marriage.

She said to Ruth, 'My daughter, I want to see you married to a good man and settled in your own home. Tonight Boaz will be celebrating the harvest at his threshing floor. Everyone will be eating and drinking. Wash yourself and make yourself beautiful. Put on your best dress and perfume and go to the threshing floor.'

'What will he think when he sees me?' asked Ruth.

'Don't let him see you,' said Naomi. 'Wait until he has finished his dinner and lies down to sleep. Then go and lie at his feet. Lift the robe from his feet and lie under it. He'll tell you what to do.'

'I'll do whatever you say,' said Ruth.

Ruth lies down at Boaz's feet

That night Boaz ate and drank well. Finally, at peace with the world, he went to sleep at the end of a heap of grain. Then, at about midnight, he woke up. As he turned over, he felt a touch on his feet. Sitting up in the darkness, he saw that a woman was lying there.

'Who are you?' he asked.

'I am your servant, Ruth,' she answered. 'Spread the corner of your robe over me, my lord, for you are my closest relative.'

Boaz understood her message. Ruth was inviting him to buy Elimelech's land and to marry her, as he had a right to do. Although he was an important man, he was pleased by her request, for she was young and beautiful and he was middle-aged.

'Bless you, my daughter,' he said. 'You are a true member of your husband's family, for you have not run after young men, rich or poor. Trust me. I will do whatever I can for you. You deserve a good husband. There is, however, a man who is more closely related to your husband's family than I am.'

He added gently, 'Spend the night here. In the morning I'll talk to him. If he wants to buy the land and marry you, he has the right to do so. If he doesn't choose to, I shall marry you, and gladly. I swear it in the name of the Lord. Now lie down and sleep.'

Boaz gives her six measures of barley

So Ruth lay at his feet until morning. Then she got up while it was still dark, for Boaz did not want anyone to see her there.

'Hold out the shawl you are wearing,' he said softly.

'When she did so, he poured six measures of barley into it and lifted it onto her back. She thanked him and, carrying the grain, returned to the town.

Naomi woke up when Ruth entered the house. 'What happened last night, my daughter?' she asked.

Ruth told her mother-in-law everything. She finished her story by saying, 'He gave me these six measures of barley as I left him. He didn't want me to return to you with empty hands.'

Naomi smiled at her. 'You have done well, Ruth. Now all we can do is wait and see what happens. I know what Boaz is like. He doesn't waste time. He'll want to settle the matter today.'

Boaz settles the matter

Boaz found the man who was Elimelech's closest relative at the town gate

'May I speak with you?' he asked.

Then, in the presence of ten other citizens, he explained the matter.

'Naomi, who has come back from the land of Moab, wants to sell the land which belonged to our relative Elimelech. You have the right to buy it if you wish,' he said. 'because you are his closest relative. If you don't wish to buy it, say so, and I'll buy it.'

'I'll buy it,' said the man.

'But,' said Boaz, 'the day you buy it, you'll also marry Ruth, the Moabite woman, the daughter-in-law of the dead man's son, Mahlon. That's what Naomi wants. In that way, the dead man's wife and his inheritance will stay together.'

Elimelech's closest relative then said, 'I can't marry Ruth without losing my own inheritance. Anyway, she's a foreigner, from Moab. I can't marry someone from Moab! You buy the land. I'll hand my rights over to you.'

He pulled off his sandal and gave it to Boaz, for this was a sign to the people that the matter was settled.

Then Boaz said to the people, 'Today you have seen that we did everything correctly, according to our customs. I'll buy the land that belonged to Elimelech. And I shall marry Ruth, the widow of Elimelech's son Mahlon. Do you agree?'

'Yes, we agree,' the people said. 'The Lord will bless you and your wife Ruth. He will build the house of Israel into a great nation through your children.'

Boaz marries Ruth

So Ruth became the wife of Boaz. Before the next harvest, she gave birth to a son. This was the child she had always wanted.

Naomi's friends said to her, 'Praise the Lord! This boy will be like another son to you, and he will be a great man in Israel. He will bring you new life and brighten your old age. For he is the child of your daughter-in-law Ruth, who loves you and is kinder to you than seven sons.'

They called the child Obed. Naomi took him in her arms and hugged him. From then on, she took great care of him.

And Obed became a great man in Israel. For the son born to Boaz and his Moabite wife, Ruth, became the grandfather of Israel's greatest king, King David.

Level 1

Adam and Eve

Noah

Jonah

Moses in Egypt

Jesus is Born

The Good Samaritan *and*
The Wise and the Foolish Bridesmaids

Level 2

Joseph

Ruth

When Jesus was a Boy

Jesus Begins God's Work
> *This story tells of the baptism and temptation of Jesus, the draught of fishes, the wedding feast at Cana, the healing of the lame man, the blessing of little children and the feeding of the five thousand.*

Lost but Found
> The Lost Sheep
> The Lost Coin
> The Prodigal Son

Jesus Dies and Lives Again